Fighting Antis

Theodor W. Adorno

Fighting Antisemitism Today

A Lecture

With an Afterword by Peter Gordon

Translated by Wieland Hoban

polity

Originally published as *Zur Bekämpfung des Antisemitismus heute. Ein Vortrag. Mit einem Nachwort von Jan Philipp Reemtsma* © Suhrkamp Verlag AG Berlin 2024. All rights reserved by and controlled through Suhrkamp Verlag AG Berlin.

This English edition © Polity Press, 2025

Polity Press
65 Bridge Street
Cambridge CB2 1UR, UK

Polity Press
111 River Street
Hoboken, NJ 07030, USA

ISBN-13: 978-1-5095-6690-7 – hardback
ISBN-13: 978-1-5095-6691-4 – paperback

A catalogue record for this book is available from the British Library.

Library of Congress Control Number: 2024942163

Typeset in 12.5 on 15 pt Adobe Garamond
by Cheshire Typesetting Ltd, Cuddington, Cheshire
Printed and bound in Great Britain by CPI Group (UK) Ltd, Croydon

For further information on Polity, visit our website:
politybooks.com

Contents

v

Introductory Note

As grateful as the author is for the initiative of the German Coordinating Council of Societies for Christian–Jewish Cooperation, which aims to make this lecture accessible to the participants of the European Educators' Conference in printed form, he is nonetheless hesitant to agree to its publication. He is aware that, in his case, the spoken and the written word diverge in their respective types of effectiveness even more than is generally the case today. If he were to speak in the same way that he is obliged to write for the sake of a rigorous factual description, the result would be incomprehensible; but no spoken words could do justice to the demands he must make of a text. The more general the objects are, the more difficult things become for someone of whom a well-meaning critic recently said that his texts follow the principle that 'the good Lord dwells in the details'. While a text has to provide exact references, lectures are necessarily restricted to the dogmatic assertion of their conclusions. Therefore, the author cannot take responsibility for what is printed here and regards it merely as an aide-mémoire for those who were present at his improvisation and would, of course, like to continue reflecting on the matters examined, based on the modest suggestions conveyed to them. To the author, the fact that there is a universal tendency to record off-the-cuff speeches on tape and then disseminate them is itself a behavioural symptom of the administered world, which seeks to pin down even that ephemeral word whose truth lies in its transience in order to commit the speaker to it. A tape recording is something akin to the fingerprint of the living spirit. The author hopes that, by making use of the German Coordinating Council's kind licence to express all of this openly, he can at least prevent some of the misinterpretations he would otherwise inevitably face.

T. W. A.

On Fighting Antisemitism Today

Ladies and gentlemen,

I feel a little as if I have been forced into the situation of Hans Sachs when he says, 'You take it lightly, but for me you make it hard; you do me, poor man, too much honour.' So you should not expect too much of what I am about to tell you.

I will quite simply restrict myself to a discussion of a few key points. I will endeavour not to say anything that will be more or less familiar to all of you but, rather, one or two things that are perhaps not so present in the general consciousness.

To speak about antisemitism and the possibility of combating it today seems a little anachronistic at first, since people generally say that antisemitism is not currently a problem in Germany. This claim is supported by the figures from opinion polls, especially the commercial polling institutes, which constantly report that the number of antisemites is in decline. The reasons for this are very tangible: firstly, the official taboos that apply to antisemitism in today's society, at least in Germany, and, secondly, the terrible fact that there are barely any Jews left in Germany who could be the objects of antisemitic prejudice. I do not intend to deny all this, but I do think that the question is not as simple as its statistical structure. You should not assume that antisemitism is an isolated, specific phenomenon. Rather, as Horkheimer and I put it in the *Dialectic of Enlightenment*, it is part of a 'ticket', a plank in a platform. Wherever people preach a certain kind of militant and excessive nationalism, antisemitism is automatically included. It has proved itself in such movements as a suitable common denominator to bring together the otherwise highly divergent forces underlying all right-wing extremism. In addition, the potential has very much survived. You need only take a look at the far-right press in Germany, which has a considerable number of representatives, to find many statements that could be declared crypto-antisemitic, and whose implications, underlined with a nod and a wink, nurture antisemitism. After all, in our work at the Frankfurt Institute of Social Research, we have good reason not to trust the pretty numbers supplied by the polling institutes without reservations. For example, it emerged in a survey some time ago that children from lower-middle-class circles, and to an extent also working-class ones, show a certain inclination towards antisemitic prejudices. We attribute this to the fact that the parents of those children belonged to the active supporters of Nazi Germany. Today they feel obliged to justify their past stance, which almost automatically leads them to warm up their antisemitism from the 1930s. Our staff member Peter Schönbach coined the rather fitting term 'secondary antisemitism' for this. Such things should be investigated. In doing so, it would be important to turn one's attention from the outset towards those groups in which this survival of fascist antisemitism can be observed. Any research in this zone must be guided by an awareness of the necessity to understand and acknowledge such phenomena and manifestations instead of being outraged by them. Only if one is capable of understanding the most extreme things – not with sympathy, but schematically – can one counteract them productively and truthfully. One symptom of the powerful collective force that is used in fending off the entire context of past guilt is the enthusiastic reception that, for some time, a number of Anglo-Saxon authors have been enjoying in Germany for their apparent exonerations of Germany in the matter of war guilt. They are eagerly quoted, even if the tenor of their books is anything but pro-German. One can probably say – reasonably assume – that, wherever such effects occur, the antisemitism of Nazi Germany is also somehow apologetically explained, out of a pure urge to collective self-defence. But as soon as one renders it plausible to oneself, for example with the argument that the influence of the Jews genuinely was excessive back then, this paves the way for a direct revival of the prejudice. Accordingly, one often hears that one should not allow the Jews – whose numbers, as I said, are truly minuscule – too much influence, that they should not have access to high positions and such like. Let me say in advance that I would consider it wrong to deny, for example, the influence of Jews in the Weimar Republic for the sake of combating antisemitism. As soon as one embarks on such casuistry, even playing around with numbers, one is already at a disadvantage. One must make the case in a far more radical way: in a democracy, any question regarding the proportions made up in different professions by different demographic groups violates the principle of equality from the outset. I say this because it strikes me as a model case for the problems we are constantly facing when arguing against antisemitism.

I drew your attention earlier to the current phenomenon of hidden antisemitism, which is a result of official taboos. This crypto-antisemitism is a function of the authority that stands behind the prohibition of open antisemitic manifestations. There is a dangerous potential in this concealment itself, however; whispers and rumours (I once called antisemitism the rumour about the Jews), opinions that are not made entirely explicit in public, have always been the medium in which different forms of social discontent that did not dare step into the light in a social order were active. Anyone who adopts such opinions or rumours immediately seems like a member of a secret, truthful community that is merely suppressed by the surface forms of society. And that is precisely the logic behind one of the central tricks used by antisemites today: to present themselves as victims of persecution; to behave as if, because public opinion makes expressions of antisemitism impossible today, it is actually the antisemite who is subject to the sting of society, whereas the antisemites are generally the ones who use the sting of society most cruelly and successfully. Crypto-antisemitism leads us automatically to the belief in authority. Now, the problem of authority plays a complex part in fighting antisemitism. One should not, for the sake of arriving at a valid formula, simplify phenomena where the realities are not simple, and indeed contradictory. One should not automatically say, 'Fighting antisemitism would mean being authoritarian, so one shouldn't use authority against antisemitism.' I can clarify the situation for you in stark terms. Of course, one should not for one second deny the close link between antisemitic prejudice and authority-bound character structures, indeed with authoritarian forces as such. In the formative processes of the personality – that is, education in the broadest possible sense – one will definitely have to counteract the formation of the authority-bound character, which means behaving in a consistently anti-authoritarian way in keeping with the results of modern pedagogy. But we are not dealing only with people whom we can educate or change but also those with whom the die has already been cast, often those for whose specific personality structure it is characteristic that they are, in a certain sense, hardened and closed to experience, not really flexible – in short, they are unresponsive. One must not dispense with authority when dealing with these people, who essentially prefer to respond to authority and whose faith in authority is very difficult to shake. Where they dare to step forward and join in openly antisemitic manifestations, the genuinely available means of power must be applied without sentimentality – not out of an urge to punish or take revenge on those people but, rather, to show them that the only thing that impresses them, namely true social authority, for the time being still stands against them after all. The arguments one puts forward against them must also be designed from the outset so that, without deviating from the truth in any way, they can reach people with such a character structure.

When I speak of authority, I cannot – especially in this company – refrain from saying a few words about the problem of religious authority too, whose invocation initially seems to be one of the most drastic means for confronting racial prejudice. I am aware that the most active and reliable forces that are in any way engaged in fighting antisemitic sentiments in Germany today often belong to religious groups, represented equally in both major Christian confessions. I hardly need to add how grateful one should be to those groups for that support. But specifically because they are so serious about fighting antisemitism and what, in a higher sense, one might call making amends, there is perhaps good reason to warn of a misunderstanding that can easily arise in the relationship between positive religion and antisemitism. For one should not take it for granted that appealing to religion automatically counteracts antisemitism; in particular, one should not infer something like a primacy of religion in fighting antisemitism simply because one belongs to a religious group, in the sense that one keeps talking about religion at every opportunity to oppose antisemites. Otherwise, one can very easily fall into what the Americans call 'preaching to the saved'. The relationship of religion to antisemitism consists in the duty to oppose it, not in a monopoly on resisting it. Here the level of awareness among antisemites themselves must be taken into account; those belonging to the core groups displaying antisemitism are unlikely to be accessible to religious arguments. Perhaps they are impressed by the power of the churches as institutions, but they generally tend towards a form of naturalist social Darwinism, as in Hitler's concoction *Mein Kampf*. The antisemitic groups largely recruited their members from social strata resisting in two directions: against socialism on the one hand and what they considered clericalism on the other hand. They exhibit both a certain opposition to conventionalist-conservative forces and an opposition to the workers. This was especially striking in Austria: anyone who was in neither the Christian Social Party nor the Social Democrats tended almost automatically towards German ethnonationalist ideology, and thus antisemitism. I presume this mentality still exists today. Basic structures of political groupings have a peculiar tenacity that apparently even survives the apocalypses we have undergone. This is why religious arguments are often at an ideological disadvantage with people who are already living in a sphere that does not allow the approach of religion and sense in it only a fictitious ultramontane claim to domination. The religious groups too should try – and this requires a certain self-renunciation – should try to fight antisemitism on its own territory. That means helping to prevent the formation of antisemitic characters on the one hand, but, where they already exist, following on from what we know about the conscious and unconscious of antisemites, to get beyond that, and not simply asserting or even propagating their position. With this we touch on the relation to the problem of propaganda in general. Allow me to preface this somewhat pointedly with a thesis: antisemitism is a *mass medium* in the sense that it taps into unconscious drives, conflicts, inclinations and tendencies that it reinforces and manipulates, instead of raising them to the conscious level and resolving them. For all its naturalism, it is a thoroughly anti-enlightening force, and has always – despite that naturalism – viewed itself in the starkest opposition to the Enlightenment, which is constantly vilified in Germany. It shares this structure with superstition, with astrology, which likewise attempts to reinforce and exploit unconscious feelings, and with all propaganda; it always does the same thing. Therefore, what we habitually call propaganda methods are automatically at a disadvantage when it comes to antisemitism. I see precisely this rational concretization of irrational tendencies, their confirmation or reproduction through different forms of mass media today, as one of the most dangerous ideological forces in contemporary society. In the context of a study attacking the commercial astrology of newspaper columns that I published some time ago, a well-known psychologist polemicized against me (without actually naming me) and accused me of taking these harmless things too seriously. He argued that it would actually be a fine thing if astrology led humans to be kind to one another and be a little more careful when driving. I do not mean to overestimate the significance of astrology, but I would also warn against underestimating it. The tendency to manipulate festering unconscious sentiments and place them in the service of some special interests, rather than resolving them, is also a factor in antisemitic prejudices. I could show you in detail that there is an exact structural correspondence between, shall we say, 'astrological stereotypes' and 'antisemitic stereotypes', and that the mechanisms in question are also the invariants of advertising psychology. One might say that antisemitism is something like the ontology of advertising. That is why, in my view, one must resist anything that resembles advertising. Whoever swims against the tide – and we must be aware that today, in the current situation, we are swimming against the tide with our work – cannot behave as if they were swimming with the tide. The only solution is emphatic enlightenment, with the whole truth, and strictly avoiding anything advert-like. Do not forget that the defensive mechanisms we must reckon with are extremely good at registering and eliminating anything advert-like. To gauge this, look at the far-right press. You are sure to find in it repeated denunciations of anything that somehow resembles advertising. (As an aside: it would be a useful form of training for our work to take a close look at the papers in question and analyse them with a view to stimuli, which they use very cleverly; we could uncover where the most sensitive zones lie today and focus our work largely on those.) There is a fundamental allergy in the populace to the advertising unleashed on the world from all sides today. But while most people are generally defenceless against it, one finds that, when it corresponds to unconscious tendencies as closely as it does in the case of antisemitism, the hostility is transferred to what one might call counter-advertising; here one encounters especially strong resistance. In their rejection of the Enlightenment, antisemites like to focus on some facts or dates that are supposedly not fully certain, such as the number of murdered Jews, the authenticity of particular documents, and so forth. It would be inherently wrong to respond to the casuistry. Instead, one should aim to bring about a reflective awareness of the manifestations of a mindset that insists there were not six but *only* five million, and which then imperceptibly progresses, as I have repeatedly been able to observe in far-right publications, to the conclusion that there were only a few thousand. In general, it is better to reveal the structures of argumentation that are brought into play than to be drawn into an endless discussion within those structures, which are laid down by the antisemites, as it were, so that one will agree a priori to play by their rules. An example: the popular approach of number games; that, yes, it is true

that an unidentified number of Jews were murdered; but 'war' – one is then told – 'is war,
splinters must fall, and Dresden, after all, was
horrific too.' No sensible person would dispute
that, but they should certainly reject this whole
way of thinking, the comparability of warfare and
a planned extermination of entire population
groups. Or: 'So much time has passed by now,
enough to finally draw a line under it'; this argument is always used by those who have the greatest
interest in drawing such a line. All one can say to
this is that, as long as a mindset like the one that
carried out the horrors survives, it is not the time
to draw that line. Or the popular argument:
'Hitler was right about so many things, such as
recognizing the danger of Bolshevism in time,
and he probably wasn't entirely wrong about the
Jews either.' Here one would have to enter into
the overall political dialectic and explain that the
terrible conflicts threatening the world today
would probably never have constituted themselves in this way had Hitler not created a situation
that led to this threat. One particularly devious
argument is this: 'You're not allowed to say anything bad about the Jews these days.' Here the
public taboo on antisemitism is specifically

turned into an argument in favour of antisemitism: if one isn't allowed to say anything bad
about the Jews, then – thus the associative logic
– there must be some truth to the bad things that
one might say about them. A projection mechanism is in operation here: that those who were
the persecutors, and potentially still are, act as if
they were the persecuted. The only way to respond
is to refrain from idealizing and singing the
praises of great Jewish men, or displaying pretty
pictures of Israeli irrigation systems or kibbutz
children, and instead explain the Jewish traits
pointed out by the antisemites, assessing their
truthfulness and accuracy. In general, rather than
making Jews harmless and presenting them as
little lambs or golden boys, it is far better to say
that they have a great, turbulent and wild history
containing just as many horrors as the histories of
other peoples. A sentimental advertising picture
would be repugnant. Nor should one, however
well-intentioned it may be, identify the Jews with
their religion, as happens so often, trying to make
them 'palatable' from the perspective of their religious deeds and achievements; it should not be
concealed that, in the bourgeois age, they were
central carriers of the Enlightenment, and one

must take a stance towards this. It is impossible to confront antisemitic potential without identifying with enlightenment. The way is not to waffle on about so-called positive achievements (as many positive achievements as there obviously are) but to address the neuralgic point itself: the critical element in the Jewish mind, which is connected to their social mobility. This critical aspect, as an aspect of truth, is indispensable to society; it was originally contained precisely in the principle of the very same bourgeois society that today, in its late phase, is seeking to dispose of the critical aspect in favour of an insipid and false ideal of positivity. Or, if I may improvise a few more such models: if antisemites say that Jews shy away from hard physical labour, it would not be the wisest solution to answer that there were many Jewish shoemakers and tailors in the East, and that there are so many Jewish taxi drivers in New York today. By speaking in this way, one already posits anti-intellectualism and thus stoops to the level of one's opponent, where one is always at a disadvantage. Instead, one should make it clear that this entire argumentation is based on resentment: one thinks one has to work hard, or does indeed have to; and because one knows deep down that hard physical work is more or less obsolete today, one denounces those of whom it is said, rightly or wrongly, that they have an easier time of it. A proper response would be that old-fashioned handiwork is superfluous today, that it has been made obsolete by technology and that there is something deeply dishonest about reproaching a particular group for not performing sufficiently hard physical labour. Developing one's intellect rather than toiling away with one's body is a human right. This would also invalidate the whole line of argumentation based on the Jews in Israel making the land fertile with the sweat of their brow. I am the last person who would diminish the remarkable achievement there. But it is itself only a reflex in response to the terrible social regression that was forced on Jews by antisemitism and must not be turned into an absolute and presented as if this sweat were something positive and meritorious in its own right. All of that requires a certain breadth, overview and assuredness that places the phenomena in context and thus, without any cheap apologetics, can at least reach anyone who is at all capable of rational thought, instead of entering into a battle of opinions in which the ones who want to defend themselves always prove weaker than the aggressive ones. I would also like to present you with a model that is very closely connected to the other one: the accusation that Jews are intermediaries. This quickly becomes an accusation of dishonesty, cheating, deception [*Täuschung*] – and indeed the latter word is related to exchanging [*Tauschen*]. One will rarely have a chance to address the full economic theory of this prejudice and how to refute it, but one can point out that, since the advent of an elaborated exchange-based bourgeois society, this intermediary function has been socially necessary. It is therefore illegitimate to denounce that function from the outset as parasitic, immoral and malign simply because it receded in the period of extreme concentration of economic power we are in today. One should also recall that there is a particular relation between the intermediary function, the sphere of circulation – as economists call it – the sphere of money and the intellect, as underlined even by a far-right thinker such as Oswald Spengler. Without the intermediary sphere, that of trading, monetary capital and mobility, the freedom of the spirit to break away from the mere immediacy of given circumstances would have been unimaginable. What I have tried to show you using these individual examples is that one can truly speak effectively against antisemitism only by telling the truth and seeing things in their complexity and their social connection with their social place, instead of sticking to cheap rebuttals that will in turn only elicit further counter-arguments and continue towards a bad infinity.

I would now like to discuss the two basic forms of resistance that I consider the decisive ones. I will simply use the American terminology, which distinguishes between the 'long-term programme' and the 'short-term programme'. These two types could also be termed the education programme and the immediate prevention programme. The difference between them is the one I suggested at the beginning: when planning for the long term one should aim to counteract the formation of authority-bound characters, whereas interventions in the present situation cannot entirely forego a certain type of authority. In the long-term programme – that is, the problem of an education that truly seeks to address the roots of antisemitism – it is important to underline something that is often misunderstood. Repeatedly, and not always in good faith, I am confronted with the argument that antisemitism is not only a psychological problem but has economic and cultural and God knows what other roots. Those of you who are somewhat familiar with the thinking I normally espouse will know that I am the last person to tend towards psychologism. Anti-Semitism cannot simply be reduced to a question of psychological attitude. But if we assume that antisemitism – or, at least, that the foundation for people to be receptive for antisemitic stimuli later on – can be attributed substantially to experiences in early childhood, then this will necessarily point towards the psychological side of things. It is precisely because this aspect is generally neglected that we placed particular emphasis on it in the study *The Authoritarian Personality*; simply to add something that is clearly less known to the many known things. But perhaps you allow me to say that elements of an *overall* theory of antisemitism in our society can be found in the book Horkheimer and I wrote, *Dialectic of Enlightenment*, and that these psychological aspects are assigned the appropriate significance there. Of course, the objectivity in which the psychological mechanisms of antisemitism are embedded naturally sets certain limits for educational work. One would be well advised not to treat these boundaries as proof that antisemitism is a primordial phenomenon; they too should be derived from social dynamics.

In the educational sphere – in the broadest sense – the aim is thus to prevent as far as possible the development of anything like an authority-bound character. I will not present the theory of that character here; there is plenty for you to read about it. But perhaps I will just remind you that repression, especially in the form of powerful, brutal paternal authority, very often produces what psychoanalysts refer to as the Oedipal character: people who are controlled on the one hand by suppressed anger but, on the other hand, because they were unable to develop, tend to identify with the authority that oppresses them and then let out their suppressed and aggressive instincts against others, generally those who are weaker. The authority-bound, specifically antisemitic character is really the 'loyal subject' portrayed by Heinrich Mann, which fawns upwards and punches downwards and displays a certain type of pseudo-rebellious mentality along the lines of 'it's high time something is done about it, someone has to finally put things in order', yet is always willing to bow to the bearers of true power, economic or otherwise, and ally itself with that power. If one examines the formation of Hitler's character, as seems to have been done in American studies, one will encounter all these things. But one should make an addition – and here I direct your attention to a problem that I urge you to reflect on, without being able to offer you an easy solution to it: the decisive element today is less the paternal brutality one finds in Hitler's case than a certain kind of coldness and lack of attachment that children experience in early childhood. This is in turn connected profoundly to the transformation of the family into a 'petrol station', as it has sometimes been called. The type of character that – if I am not mistaken – is psychologically threatening today in our context is far more like what I call the manipulative type in *The Authoritarian Personality*. Examples are pathically cold, socially disconnected, mechanically administering individuals like Himmler and the camp commander Hoess. It is extremely difficult to counteract the formation of this type in early childhood. It is a reaction to a lack of affect, and one cannot preach affect. That freedom of affect does not come about is the fault of our society itself. This is one of the objective limits of psychological education that I pointed out to you earlier. It is an especially critical zone; one should think very carefully about what one can do in it without descending into the mendacity of synthetic nest warmth, nest warmth with air conditioning – just as there is nothing more foolish than ordering people to love.

The following remarks relate to my own experiences and make no claims to strict scientific dignity, but they can at least be meaningfully integrated into the scientific conception of the authority-bound character. The origins of antisemitism in early childhood can generally be found in the *family home*. Usually, everything has already been decided by the time a child begins school. It is a secondary source; antisemitic schoolmates will have been inculcated with antisemitism at home and then often occupy a key position of sorts in school. As I touched on earlier, there is a particular danger from those parents who seek to justify themselves to their children for their own National Socialist past and therefore tend to warm up self-exculpatory antisemitic arguments that are adopted by the children. It would be of great importance to contact and appeal to parents of children as early as the kindergarten phase should one observe any signs of ethnocentric reactions, also towards negro children (the structures of these phenomena are completely identical; I cannot emphasize this strongly enough). However, there is a danger that these parents themselves are fixed in their antisemitism and cannot be genuinely convinced. In such cases, it would be advisable to select precisely those children who are already inculcated with or susceptible to antisemitism and speak to them individually. A plausible hypothesis is that these would be children who have been repressed or treated especially coldly. If one were to address their individual needs, if one could soften their hardness, one could probably reach them, since they would be receiving that which they unconciously need. In addition, the respective educators would truly have to be capable in some way of giving the children what they lack at home – and the entire problem lies in what 'in some way' means. I would also assume that one is here dealing consistently, from kindergarten and then in school, with a key group comprising only a few children – one might, to use a familiar expression in an unfamiliar context, call them 'public opinion leaders'. One should concentrate the informative and educational work on them from the outset, instead of spreading education in this area broadly and hence without the appropriate intensity. One should concentrate one's attention on them and try to change them. In cases where there is strong resistance from home, an educator should not shy away from conflicts with the parents. The educator should teach the children that what they hear at home is not God's truth, that their parents can be wrong and why. One should expect educators to have the necessary civil courage for such conflicts.

I consider it possible that there is a critical moment in the formation of the authority-bound character and antisemitic prejudice. If I am not mistaken, that moment – and I offer this as a proposition that the pedagogues among you will be able to verify or falsify – is when a child begins school. That moment, you see, is the first time one enters a secondary group that is cold and unfamiliar, when one loses that nest warmth – if such a thing still exists today – in a sudden, almost shock-like way. The trauma this creates can easily solidify antisemitic notions. Pressure and coldness the child has experienced are passed on; because one suddenly feels excluded, one wishes to exclude others too and looks for suitable candidates. Educators should turn their attention to this shock moment and pre-empt it if possible. It used to be a popular custom, especially in rural schools, for the teacher to give the new children pretzels, which he had actually received secretly from the parents. The pretzel custom offers quite a profound insight into the phenomenon. One should follow this archaic model and seek to prevent the shock of the cold and thus a turn towards aggression; in other words, during the first weeks of school, one should adapt the pretzel custom to a form of behaviour that makes school lessons as much like play as possible. First one would need to carry out a systematic investigation of the entire complex, doing something like social research in schools, before one could devise truly concise measures. But one never knows how much time one has in such delicate matters. My tendency, if these tentative observations of mine are plausible, would therefore be to try out practical steps.

One should generally investigate the problem of *exclusion* in school, the formation of particular groups or cliques that are almost always held together by being directed against others who are not allowed to join in: 'I'm not playing with you', or 'That boy, nobody plays with him'. This phenomenon is essentially built in the same way as antisemitism. The opposite form of human relationship would be not some vague collective classroom community but, rather, individual friendship. A pedagogy designed to counteract prejudice would aim to encourage individual friendships and not, as certainly still occurs often in school, to treat them with sarcasm and denigration; as far as possible, it should work against the formation of whispering cliques and such groups, especially when they seek to gain control in any way. The structure of clique formation in school in general is a key phenomenon; it constitutes something like a microcosm of society as a whole. Clearly, cliques are based on a form of secret hierarchy that is opposed to the official school hierarchy, which is determined by performance. It rewards entirely different attributes – physical strength, certain kinds of skill and the like – that are neglected elsewhere. In this context one should point out the danger from organizations outside schools that approach the children and are joined by some children but not by others. This can easily become a principle of exclusion, depending in part on the ideological content of such organizations. Children with a particular tendency to form such cliques, and among them the leaders of those cliques, will also often tend towards antisemitism and indeed be the antisemitic public opinion leaders. Their opinion is a precursor to the later 'non-public' one. It is fundamentally necessary to take a very close look at the type of the child inculcated with antisemitism; analysing the character structure of this type would help to develop the character of these children in a different way. Susceptible children will often be found among those whom, very much in a metaphorical sense, I call the 'classroom proletariat' – that is, the small group of very badly performing pupils who are picked on a priori by the teachers, who quiz them with the clearly visible expectation of a wrong answer; they are also excluded from the official school hierarchy in a number of other ways. In general, they are pushed to transfer their own situation to others, to cast other children out. If I am not mistaken in my observations, these are not infrequently quite talented children, by no means dunces; they are talented in a practical, realistic sense but unable to make any progress with their talents – very much like those people who, despite having a certain organizational talent and some abilities, were unsuccessful but immediately rose up with the start of the Third Reich, when they were able to achieve something and truly have at it. More than a few of these children are likely to come from a milieu in which they were left behind, as the saying goes. In school, inhibitions prevent them from showing what they are really capable of, although they feel the potential within themselves. Their bottled-up resentment is then directed at others. Of course, antisemitic potential will be very common among unruly, refractory children, among those who also tend towards violence and sadism in other ways. They often hold leading positions in the unofficial classroom hierarchy.

Where attempts to influence them individually prove unsuccessful, one will probably have to confront them with authority in school; one must make their ideological effect on the others punishable and then carry out those punishments too. However, it is more important to get these children to speak, for them to learn to express themselves, by no means only for the cathartic effect of language in general. Those children – again, this is only based on memories and observations – often resent those who can speak, who can express themselves. It would ultimately be one of the most important and decent methods in the fight against antisemitism to increase the capacity for expression in general and mitigate the resentment about speaking. I think that student councils, the election of student representatives – all these institutions, and student parliaments too, would have the urgent task of helping children to articulate themselves and of breaking the children's taboo on the ability to speak. Children who denounce someone with the ability to speak as a toady are automatically potential recruits for antisemitic prejudice. For them, skill and practical sense are opposed to the intellect. I know of few documents that are as typical for the formation of the antisemitic character as one that I recall very well, but which, as far as I know, has been entirely forgotten: an edict that Hitler issued in the first months after coming to power in 1933. One of its stipulations is that Jewish children must on no account be top of the class any longer. Here the Nazis, with their instinct for these complexes, touched on a foundational layer of antisemitism, namely resentment of the intellect, which overtaxes children and often cannot mean anything to them in the form of traditional education. Preventive work also includes doing away with the tacit identification of Jews with intellect. Freedom in the relationship between Germans and Jews would also involve no longer assuming automatically that all Jews are clever; some are stupid. If it becomes clear that intelligence is not an attribute of a particular group or race or religion but only the quality of individuals, this will already be some help.

One should equally counteract so-called positive stereotyping, for negative stereotypes lurk closely behind it. If someone says, 'The Jews are all so clever', then, even if it is said as praise, that person is only a small step away from 'and that's why they want to cheat us'. One should also be suspicious towards statements such as 'The Jews are such a strange, special, profound people'. My friend Nevitt Sanford replied humorously to the antisemitic stereotype 'Some of my best friends are Jews' with the remark 'Some of my worst enemies are Jews'. Emancipation from forming stereotypes about the group as such is probably a more effective way of opposing prejudice than mechanically replacing a negative prejudice with a positive one. It is collective characterizations as such, which are disastrously common in Germany about all manner of groups, that must be eliminated; one certainly cannot correct one false collective characterization with a different, equally false one.

One last word on the role of the teacher in combating antisemitism. I suspect that a considerable number of teachers still sympathize silently, tacitly, non-explicitly with antisemitism. It is precisely by refraining from saying this openly, only hinting at it in an almost imperceptible, gestural way, that they establish a kind of agreement with the susceptible students from the outset. Those students then have the feeling that they finally have some social authority behind them. They feel secured and strengthened. I said earlier that vague hints are typical of antisemitism as long as it is not in power, that the hint can sometimes be a more dangerous form than an open expression. I would not presume to stipulate any rules about this, much less to recommend particular tests. One should, however, develop criteria for selecting teachers that make it possible to exclude from the start those who sympathize with the authoritarian character, and thus with antisemitism. I recall one very dark-haired teacher from my own school – he could easily have been taken for a Jew, without incidentally being notable in his academic achievements; there is no teacher from whom I learnt as little as I did from him, although he never did me any wrong. But he maintained a certain kind of camaraderie with the students and was very popular with them, a 'hail fellow well met' type of man. Around the end of the First World War, I was very surprised to hear him come out with antisemitic diatribes, though this did not prevent him, with his dashing duelling scar and socialite airs, from marrying the daughter of a rich Jew shortly afterwards. I have no idea what became of the marriage. He embodied school itself in a demagogic way, a sort of failed existence. Such social characters among teachers – which I do not view only negatively, I might add – would merit study. I would be especially glad to discuss the question of selecting teachers, which is naturally very difficult, especially because of the danger of denunciation and opinion snooping. I can only point out a very serious problem, not claim to have the solution. I suppose that would really be a matter for genuine pedagogical circles. It is precisely the sentiment 'You can't say anything these days' – that is, sympathy with non-public opinion – that will bring types like that teacher together with the latent class hierarchy of the strong, realistic, anti-intellectual fellows. This results in a conspiratorial community of the most threatening kind.

Let me conclude with some very brief remarks on the question of a short-term programme. As I have already said, I do not think much of establishing so-called contacts or such like with people in whom the prejudice has already taken root. Their capacity for experience has already been dulled. One must oppose antisemitic statements very energetically: they must see that those who challenge them have no fear. A vicious dog is impressed as soon as it realizes that one is not afraid of it, but one is lost if it senses that one trembles at the sight of its maw; it is the same in those cases. I had direct experiences with such people after returning to Germany. On one occasion I walked past a group of chauffeurs who belonged to the pool of people working for the American occupation forces. They were viciously cursing the Jews among themselves. I went to the nearest policeman and had them arrested. At the police station I had a long, in-depth conversation with the ringleader in particular, and he said something that stuck in my memory: 'You know, yesterday we were Nazis, today we're Yanks and tomorrow we'll be commies.' With those words, he unintentionally gave me a profound insight into the whole character structure of his type. For him, adapting at any cost outweighs all other motives. If one engages without fear in such cases and answers these people's arguments quite frankly, one can achieve something. I had the feeling, at any rate, that those chauffeurs left the police station with a slightly different attitude, at least in terms of their conscious convictions. When one encounters explicit and fixed prejudices, one must trust in a form of shock therapy. One must adopt the most starkly opposed positions; shock and moral strength go hand in hand in such cases. The worst thing is to relent. Someone who has little in common with the authority-bound character is especially unlikely to insist on the implementation of punishments and so forth; for those like us, any form of what Americans call 'punitiveness' is repulsive. But showing humanity is usually interpreted as a sign of weakness or a guilty conscience and activates the mechanism of blackmail. One must take care both in one's behaviour and one's argumentation that one does not trigger the stereotype of weakness, which prejudiced people use against those with a different point of view. And one genuinely has to assert one's arguments. For example, if someone says 'There's no smoke without fire' (if there is so much antisemitism, the Jews must be at least partly responsible), then one must elucidate how this saying serves as a defence through displacement, that it is not truth but ideology. With prejudiced people, who usually pick out a particular form of realism and insist ruthlessly on individual and national self-interest, one should bring up the demonstrable and visible consequences of National Socialism. They should be reminded of where it all leads, and what would most likely happen to them under a new regime of wholesale fascism or semi-fascism. With these people, who, as I say, are often far from stupid, merely hardened and stubborn, one should also refer to the fact that no one in our society likes to be taken for a fool. One must demonstrate that the entire spirit of antisemitism is indeed, as the famous quotation goes, the socialism of fools, that they are talked into it in order to be transformed into objects of manipulation. That is the simple truth, and it should certainly not fail to make an impression if one meets the prejudiced individuals on the level of their own somewhat overstated realism; if one convinces them that they are achieving the opposite of what they actually expect, that would be very fruitful. At the moment, antisemitic feeling is further nourished by a particular situation; I am referring to the anti-American affect. If I am not mistaken, it has been growing since the Berlin crisis, since everyone noticed that things are not all rosy between Washington and Bonn. People are striking up the old lament 'We're being betrayed, we're being left in the lurch', evidently in whispering campaigns too. The call of 'Betrayal, betrayal' has proved extremely demagogically effective on both sides of the Rhine. Now that the current American government is a left-wing government and Kennedy seems to have a number of Jewish advisers, it makes sense that the flourishing of the anti-Kennedy complex should secretly be accompanied by that of the antisemitic one. Effective prevention of antisemitism is inseparable from a prevention of nationalism in all its forms. One cannot be against antisemitism on the one hand while being a militant nationalist on the other. A rational attitude in matters of world politics instead of an ideological and resentment-filled nationalism is probably the most essential requirement for improvement. In the current moment, this is closely connected to the reawakening of anti-intellectualism. One finds it at every turn nowadays – and certainly not only among right-wing extremists but extending far into the manifestations of a so-called moderate conservatism. This is connected to the German form of conformism. I know that the anti-intellectuals become particularly enraged when they hear the word 'conformism', but this anger at the word shows precisely how powerful the phenomenon is, that conformism is still dutifully rendering its service. Once a group opinion has been established, any deviation from it is automatically considered disturbing and questionable. Here it is especially important who points out the deficiencies of a system or the problems of a particular state of affairs. That person – according to the betrayal model – is held responsible for the deficiencies, and thus the state of affairs they describe is exonerated. The remark by old Helvetius that the truth has not harmed anyone except those who utter it still holds today. People need to be made aware of this mechanism. One should not shrink back in the face of anti-intellectual arguments, not make any concessions to them, but rather challenge them directly with militant enlightenment. That is, one should say that in a universal constitution of humanity, and also the German nation, in which people's consciousness is no longer shackled and deformed by all manner of influencing mechanisms, being intellectual would no longer be an envied and consequently vilified privilege; instead, all people essentially could and even should be what is generally reserved for intellectuals. Moreover, the images used to incite against intellectuals used by many of the mass media, and by no means primarily in Germany, are often simply thinly veiled antisemitic stereotypes. One should talk to the film industry so that they avoid such anti-intellectual stereotypes because of those implications. They are by no means restricted to the culture industry, however, but also haunt so-called high culture. I once showed that, in one of the most famous works of German opera theatre, *Die Meistersinger*, the glaringly negative figure of

Beckmesser, although he obviously cannot be a Jew since he is a member of a guild, is characterized in a way that incorporates every conceivable antisemitic stereotype. It would be particularly necessary to point this out and detoxify it in the context of a certain traditional, established German culture. I hardly dare imagine how much damage is still being done today by books such as Gustav Freytag's *Debt and Credit*. Respect for our so-called cultural heritage should not prevent us from looking closely at it. Antisemitism was not suddenly injected into German culture from without by Hitler; rather, this culture was already riddled with antisemitic prejudices, even where it considered itself most cultivated.

Racial prejudice of every variety is archaic today, and in glaring contradiction to the reality in which we live. Nonetheless, we cannot neglect a fact recently pointed out at the philosophers' meeting in Münster by a sociological-philosophical thinker: the more such unrealities lose any real basis in an increasingly rationalized and technological civilization, the more one sees a simultaneous growth in the irrational tendency to maintain them, to cling to them. Now, once one becomes aware of this contradiction and then conveys it to others, one can genuinely proceed according to a principle that probably cannot be captured more truthfully than in the resolution: 'Such a thing must never happen again.'

Editor's Note

Theodor W. Adorno gave the lecture 'Zur Bekämpfung des Antisemitismus heute' on 2 November 1962 at the invitation of the German Coordinating Council of Societies for Christian–Jewish Cooperation (specifically Leopold Goldschmidt) for the First European Pedagogical Conference, which took place in Wiesbaden from 30 October to 3 November 1962. For its first printing in 1963, in the conference volume *Erziehung vorurteilsfreier Menschen* [Educating people to be free of prejudice] published by the coordinating council, Adorno slightly revised the transcript of the lecture. The present text is based on the reprint in Theodor W. Adorno, *Gesammelte Schriften*, ed. Rolf Tiedemann, in collaboration with Gretel Adorno, Susan Buck-Morss and Klaus Schultz, vol. 20.1: *Vermischte Schriften I* (Frankfurt am Main: Suhrkamp, 1986), pp. 360–83. What appears there as footnote 1 now forms the 'Introductory Note' (p. 0), following an early reprint in *Das Argument* 29, vol. 6 (1964), pp. 88–104 (part 2).

Afterword:
Reading Adorno on Antisemitism Today
Peter Gordon

Theodor Adorno's lecture on the task of combating antisemitism, published here for the first time in an entirely new English translation, was first presented in the West German town of Wiesbaden in November 1962 in a meeting organized by the German Coordinating Council of Societies for Christian–Jewish Cooperation (*Deutscher Koordinierungsrat der Gesellschaften für Christlich-Jüdische Zusammenarbeit*, or DKR), a group that was founded in 1949 in the wake of the Holocaust with the express purpose of promoting interfaith dialogue.[1] The specific occasion for the 1962 meeting was the 'First European Pedagogical Conference', the proceedings of which were assembled and published the following year in a volume with the hopeful title *Erziehung vorurteilsfreier Menschen* (which we might loosely translate as 'Education for a humanity free of prejudice').[2] Although more than sixty years have passed since its initial publication, the lecture retains its relevance today, not least for the dismaying reason that, despite a great many educational programmes that have the stated objective of eradicating prejudice, anti-semitism itself has hardly disappeared.

For Adorno himself the problem had never ceased to be a major concern for reasons both personal and political. The son of Oscar Wiesengrund, a successful German-Jewish wine seller, Theodor Adorno was raised in a Frankfurt milieu with a great many Jewish friends and colleagues but never felt a strong identity as a Jew, and as an adult he opted to assume the last name of his Catholic mother Maria Calvelli-Adorno. However, his self-conception as a person without ethno-religious attachment could not save him from the definitions imposed in 1933 by the laws of the Third Reich, according to which he was a so-called *Mischling* (or person of mixed racial descent) and thus ineligible for a career as a professor in Germany. His father Oscar suffered a brutal beating by the Gestapo but eventually escaped together with Maria and ultimately landed in the United States. His friend Walter Benjamin, who tried to escape fascism through a treacherous route in the Pyrenees, had been the beneficiary of financial support from the Institute of Social Research. When Adorno learnt of his friend's desperate act of suicide, he was left for the remainder of his life with what he called 'the drastic guilt of the spared'.[3] Such feelings of moral responsibility are transcribed into nearly everything that Adorno wrote after the war. In *Negative Dialectics*, his late masterpiece of philosophy, he confesses that he cannot overcome the sense of belonging to a ghostlike tribe who are 'secretly haunted by dreams in which they no longer live, but were gassed in 1944, as if their entire existence after that was purely imaginary, an emanation of the vagrant wish of someone who was killed twenty years ago.'[4]

But the problem of antisemitism for Adorno was not simply a biographical concern. As a social philosopher whose thinking bears the deep imprint of the German Idealist and left-Hegelian inheritance, Adorno believed that no society is rational if it permits social injustice to persist. In *The Holy Family*, Marx and Engels had declared that 'states which cannot yet *politically* emancipate the Jews must be rated by comparison with the perfected political state and shown to be under-developed states.'[5] Not unlike Marx, Adorno remained faithful to the emancipatory promise of the Enlightenment despite its dialectical regression into unreason. Even the catastrophe of the Nazi genocide, with its superficially rationalized techniques of mass murder, did not move Adorno to a thoroughgoing rejection of the Enlightenment itself. In his 1958 lecture series 'Introduction to Dialectics', he allowed that 'we must constantly recognize the dialectic of enlightenment.' Although we cannot ignore 'all the sacrifice and injustice which the enlightenment has brought in its course'. He explained that these contradictions show how the enlightenment has betrayed its very own promise and has revealed '*that it is still partial, as actually not yet enlightened enough* [als eine noch partielle, also nicht aufgeklärt genug].'[6] Rather than condemning the enlightenment, he declared that 'it is only by pursuing *the enlightenment's own principle* through *to its end* that these wounds may perhaps be healed.'[7]

Adorno's lifelong interest in the problem of antisemitism is grounded in the conviction that it is the symptom of deeper social pathologies. In the 1962 lecture he states that antisemitism has always stood 'in the starkest opposition to the Enlightenment'. Not unlike Marx, he notes that, in bourgeois society, Jews were 'central carriers of the Enlightenment' thanks in part to their social mobility and the 'critical element' that emerged in the European Jewish spirit during the era of emancipation. Antipathy to the Jews can therefore be understood as an irrational reflex that turns in fury against not only the Jews but all those who promote critical reason. The species of stereotypical thinking exemplified by anti-semitic prejudice also appears in astrology and in the mass media; in all of these cases we find an irrational substitution whereby ready-made categories of mythical symbolism weaken and eventually threaten to destroy the capacity for genuine reflection. Antisemitism is therefore (in Adorno's words) 'something like the ontology of advertising'.

Such broad characterizations, however, would hardly suffice to explain what is most instructive in the lecture. Animating this relatively brief commentary is an attempt to combine socio-logical insights with categories borrowed from psychoanalysis. This combination was to remain a distinguishing mark of Frankfurt School criti-cal theory, especially among representatives of the 'first generation'. Already in his 1924 thesis (completed at the University of Frankfurt) Adorno had sought to bring Freudian and Marxist theory into dialectical contact, though without reducing the independent explanatory force of either one to the other. With the rise of fascism it seemed altogether obvious that tra-ditional methods of political analysis could no longer suffice. After all, fascism appeared both modern *and* primitive – a regressive (or at least pseudo-regressive) resurgence of irrational group solidarity under seemingly rational conditions of modern civilization. Without abandoning their basic commitments to neo-Marxist modes of explanation, many of the Institute's leading members (including Adorno, Horkheimer, Erich Fromm and Herbert Marcuse) turned to psycho-analysis in order to comprehend the unfolding catastrophe.[8]

Adorno himself was drawn more deeply into psychoanalytic methods when he joined colleagues from the University of California at Berkeley in the landmark project in social psychology that was published in 1950 as *The Authoritarian Personality*. Together with R. Nevitt Sanford (a professor of psychology at Berkeley), Else Frenkel-Brunswik (a Vienna-trained psychoanalyst and a refugee from fascism) and Daniel J. Levinson (who had recently completed his dissertation in psychology at Berkeley), Adorno sought to develop qualitative and quantitative metrics for assessing the susceptibility of average Americans to fascist propaganda. Using both questionnaires and personal interviews, the study hypothesized the existence of an 'authoritarian' personality type that already takes shape in early childhood. An authoritarian personality consists in a complex of tendencies such as conventionalism, submissiveness, stereotypy (or a 'disposition to think in rigid categories') and a general preoccupation with 'toughness'.[9]

It is important to note that the features that comprise the 'F-scale' are not explicitly ideological; the study's stated purpose, after all, was to discover a strong correlation between overt commitment to ideological doctrine and a latent inclination to fascism that inheres in the structure of the individual personailty. Those who scored high on the F-scale would also exhibit high scores in overtly political ideologies such as ethnocentrism and antisemitism. In developing the antisemitism (or 'A-S') scale, Adorno translated some of the philosophical insights that he and Horkheimer had sketched out just a few years earlier in the chapter on 'Elements of antisemitism' in their co-authored *Dialectic of Enlightenment*. Adorno's biographer Stefan Müller-Doohm has even proposed that we read *The Authoritarian Personality* as 'a continuation of the *Dialectic of Enlightenment* by other means'.[10]

The 1962 lecture on combating antisemitism refers in numerous places to the substantive discoveries of *The Authoritarian Personality*. Adorno suggests, for example, that an individual who is inclined to antisemitism will tend to exhibit a 'specific personality structure' that is 'hardened and closed to experience'. Such an individual will tend to be generally inflexible or 'unresponsive' (*unansprechbar*). It should not surprise us that these are qualities that also appear with great prominence elsewhere in Adorno's philosophical reflections on the pathologies of modern society.[11] He expressed a special concern at the emergence of 'bourgeois coldness' as the modern subject gradually lost its capacity for experience and grew increasingly indifferent to both the singularity of other individuals and the sensuous particularity of the surrounding world.[12]

Because the lineaments of the authoritarian personality are formed in the experiences of early childhood, we should not be surprised to find that in the lecture on combating antisemitism Adorno places special emphasis on childhood experiences, especially in early education. In a reflection from *Minima Moralia* entitled 'The bad comrade' that was written during the years 1946–7, Adorno observed that 'I ought to be able to deduce fascism from the memories of my childhood.'[13] His comments turn especially on the habits of clique formation among children and their penchant to turn all of their aggression upon those who are deemed outsiders or excessively intellectual. In Adorno's analysis, even the most casual remark of one child to another, 'I'm not playing with you', appears as the cruel seed from which later exclusions will grow.

Adorno's remarks on the dynamics of group psychology draw much of their inspiration from earlier studies in crowd behaviour, such as Gustav Le Bon's *The Crowd* (originally published in French as *Pyschologie des foules*, 1985) and Freud's reflections on social irrationality and aggression in works such as *Beyond the Pleasure Principle* (1920) and *Group Psychology and the Analysis of the* Ego (1921). It was one of the prominent themes of psychoanalytic theory (especially following Europe's descent into the nationalist violence of the First World War) that no social group is entirely innocent: all instances of nationalist and group solidarity have the potential to revive the atavistic passions that Freud ascribed to the 'primal horde'.[14] While the individual exhibits restraint, the group threatens to dissolve the individual into an irrational collective that acts on the basis of shared emotion. The result is 'a regression to an earlier stage such as we are not surprised to find among savages or children.'[15] Such themes form the theoretical foundation for Adorno's reflections on antisemitism, which he calls a '*mass medium*' because 'it taps into unconscious drives, conflicts, inclinations and tendencies' whose power over the individual it both manipulates and enhances. In his lecture the formation of the authoritarian personality in early childhood receives unusual emphasis: Adorno returns several times to the insight that the formation of cliques among schoolchildren will tend to reward those who are inclined towards 'violence and sadism'. In this respect, this penchant for clique formation resembles 'a microcosm of society as a whole'. Even Adorno's rather amusing suggestion that schoolchildren should be given pretzels reflects his belief, as stated in the conclusion to *The Authoritarian Personality*, that the remedy to social pathologies such as antisemitism lies on a deeper stratum than mere ideology: '*All that is really essential is that children be genuinely loved and treated as individual humans.*'[16]

In reading the lecture, we should note that Adorno does not single out antisemitism as a wholly unique phenomenon; he never succumbs to the now commonplace opinion that antisemitism ranks as the *summum malum* or culminating evil of modern civilization. On the contrary, he sees it as one instance of a general rule of group solidarity, namely that identification nearly always presupposes exclusion. The warm feeling of a collective bond – whether it is based on mythic claims to ethno-religious, national or racial identity – gains its reality only by expelling from the group those who bear the stigma of difference. In one striking passage, Adorno hastens to explain that, as early as kindergarten, educators must guard against a tendency to ethnocentric reactions 'also towards negro children'. In a parenthetical remark he adds that 'the structures of these phenomena are completely identical; I cannot emphasize this strongly enough.'

The deep logic of the lecture on antisemitism must therefore be read against the background of a principled commitment to universalism. It is, however, a universalism torn by disappointment, since Adorno recognizes that Enlightenment principles have failed again and again to realize their promise. As he acknowledges elsewhere in his writing, even the most idealistic artefacts of modern culture tend to lapse into a bad dialectic. In a comment on the text by Schiller that Beethoven set to music for the finale to the Symphony in D Minor (Opus 125) Adorno observes with some bitterness: 'It is peculiar to the bourgeois Utopia that it is not yet able to conceive an image of perfect joy without that of the person excluded from it: it can take pleasure in that image only in proportion to the unhappiness in the world.'[17] No matter how compromised the Enlightenment's ideals may be, however, Adorno never rejects these ideals entirely. He continued to believe in universalist standards of democratic equality and inclusion. To overcome prejudice in all its forms, he goes so far as to endorse what he calls 'militant enlightenment' that would be secured by nothing less than 'a universal constitution of humanity' [*Gesamtverfassung der Menschheit*].

One should not lose sight of the political anxieties in the early years of the German Federal Republic that moved Adorno to issue such muscular statements. In his view, the defeat of the Third Reich did not signify the defeat of the deeper forces that had made Nazism possible. In a newly reconstructed public sphere that was determined to repress, or at least remain silent about, the crimes of the previous regime, any candid expression of anti-democratic sentiment and prejudice was widely considered taboo. But, in the group psyche, what is rendered taboo does not disappear; it is only pushed underground where it results in collective neurosis, or what the German psychoanalysts Alexander and Margarete Mitscherlich in their 1967 study called 'the inability to mourn'.[18] In his many lectures, both in public and on the radio, Adorno frequently admonished his German audiences that they should not ignore the political pathologies that are born from repression; they must instead confront the challenging task of *Trauerarbeit*, or 'working through the past'. In a well-known lecture on this topic from 1959, he warned that 'I consider the survival of National Socialism *within* democracy to be potentially more menacing than the survival of fascist tendencies *against* democracy.' Over the next two decades his fears would prove well-founded; an insurgent block of post-fascists, newly named the National Democratic Party, would succeed in surpassing the 5 per cent threshold of votes to secure official representation in no fewer than seven of Germany's regional parliaments.[19] Until the end of his life Adorno did not cease to issue warnings about the persistence of antisemitic and fascist forces in West German political culture.

Nor should we forget the war-crime trials of the early 1960s that drew attention both in Germany and abroad. The trial of Adolf Eichmann in Jerusalem began in April 1961 and concluded when the defendant was sentenced to death in mid-December that same year. During his late spring and summer 1965 lectures on metaphysics,

Adorno commented on Hannah Arendt's controversial statement that Eichmann exemplified 'the banality of evil'. Although on philosophical matters Adorno and Arendt seldom agreed, he shared her basic view of modern evil as characterized by banality or (in his words) 'triviality' [*das Triviale*]. But he hastened to add a small correction: 'I would not say that evil is trivial, but that triviality is evil.'[20] The claim was already familiar to readers of *The Authoritarian Personality*: the atrocities of modern society could not be blamed on a handful of antisemitic fanatics alone; they were due to everyday patterns of conventionalism and obedience that were widespread in the human psyche. The general thesis also aligned with the findings of the Yale psychologist Stanley Milgram, whose 1961 experiments in obedience appeared to show that a readiness to follow orders could move ordinary people to extraordinary acts of cruelty.[21]

Much closer to home were the Auschwitz trials that convened in Frankfurt between December 1963 and August 1965, in which twenty-two defendants stood accused of murder. Fritz Bauer, the attorney general of the state of Hessen, had hoped that the trial might serve as a 'public history lesson'.[22] But when the trial came to an end he felt grave disappointment. In prosecuting a discrete set of individuals he feared that the trials had nourished what he called the 'wishful fantasy that there were only a few people with responsibility', as if 'the rest were merely terrorized, violated hangers-on, compelled to do things completely contrary to their true nature.'[23] In his view, the trial had obscured the far more unsettling truth that moral responsibility was not simply a matter of individual conduct but was distributed across all modern society. By coincidence, Adorno lived not far from Bauer in Frankfurt's West End and admired him for his 'moral courage'. In July 1968, when he learnt of the judge's death, Adorno paused from his lectures on sociology to offer a few words of praise: 'I know of very few people who have worked with such passion and such energy to ensure that calamity is not repeated in Germany and that fascism in all its menacing guises is resisted.'[24]

At the time that the Auschwitz trials were under way in Frankfurt, Adorno was offering a lecture series on problems of moral philosophy. Adorno shared Bauer's general opinion that moral blame was as much systemic as individual.

This was a lesson that applied not only to the murder of European Jewry but to all comparable atrocities of the modern era. In sum, Adorno saw in Auschwitz not an exemption to rationalized modernity but an exemplum. In the extremity of its horror, it revealed horrors that were no longer extreme but sedimented into the institutional and quotidian features of modern life. In his 1965 lectures on metaphysics, he observed that the name of Auschwitz 'stands for something unthinkable beyond the unthinkable, namely, *a whole historical phase*' [*eine ganze geschichtliche Phase*].[25] The question of whether moral philosophy is 'possible today' was therefore the question of whether morality could retain any validity under historical conditions that had made moral transgression commonplace.[26] The 1962 lecture on combating antisemitism is perhaps best read as a supplement to these academic lectures. But we should also read it alongside Adorno's various other public speeches of the postwar era. These include his 1967 speech in Vienna on 'The New Right-Wing Extremism' and his series of conversations, recorded for German radio between 1959 and 1969, that were published posthumously under the title *Education for Maturity*.[27]

The German word for maturity, *Mündigkeit*, merits further consideration, since it alerts us to Adorno's enduring commitment in a standard of Enlightenment reason that has its roots in Kantian idealism. Antisemitism clearly violates this rational standard. It is not a self-consistent ideology let alone a suite of ideas; it is best understood as a protean attitude that is essentially *irrational* and flexible in its uses. To borrow a term from Jean-Paul Sartre that Adorno found apt, antisemitism is a *passion*.[28] Because it has no fixed content, antisemitism can serve a wide variety of purposes, and it can even function, paradoxically, without reference to Jews: it becomes the changeable concatenation of half-conscious beliefs and symbols that the historian Shulamith Volkov has called a 'cultural code'.[29] This is what Adorno and Horkheimer had in mind when they defined it in *Dialectic of Enlightenment* as only one component in the 'ticket' thinking of mass-political ideology; or, as Adorno says in the lecture, it is merely 'a plank in a platform'.

The irrational and variable character of antisemitism makes it especially resistant to rational refutation. According to Adorno, even the ostensibly philosemitic appeal to counter-examples – such as idealizing images of Israelis as 'golden boys' who live on the kibbutz – tends to reinforce the old prejudice that there was some truth to the old caricature of the hyper-intellectual Jew of the diaspora who did not earn his living by the sweat of his brow. Although Adorno does not express the point directly, those who know the history of Zionism will immediately recognize the veracity in his claim: much of the power of Zionist ideology lay in its promise to 'negate the diaspora', and that meant granting legitimacy to the old canard that there was something wrong with the way that the Jewish people had been living before their political transformation into people who could claim for themselves the safety and strength of belonging to their own nation-state. Adorno denies this bad dualism: instead of seeking to refute antisemitic prejudice by pointing to so-called good Jews who falsify the stereotype, one should resist stereotypical thinking altogether. This means overcoming the allure of 'collective characterizations'. As Adorno notes, 'one certainly cannot correct one false collective characterization with a different, equally false one.'

This may rank as the single most important theme in Adorno's lecture. It drives home the point that his topic is far more expansive than antisemitism itself, since the forces that animate antisemitism reappear elsewhere in human behaviour, in other prejudices and other exclusions. The closing line of the lecture is that 'Such a thing must never happen again.' This closely anticipates one of the most forceful phrases in the concluding chapter of *Negative Dialectics*, where Adorno wrote that 'Hitler has imposed a new categorical imperative upon humanity in the state of their unfreedom: to arrange their thinking and conduct, so that Auschwitz never repeats itself, so that nothing similar ever happens again.' The operative terms in this imperative are 'similar' and 'again'.[30] It should be altogether obvious that the logic of similarity and the possibility of comparison in human affairs underwrites all international law. Taken together, these words deny the uniqueness of anti-Jewish prejudice and even the singularity of the Shoah: they speak to the terrible fact that, in its capacity for collective murder, humanity shows no limit in its inventiveness or its choice of victims.[31]

Today the question of antisemitism has become a point of political contestation as perhaps never before. Whether a given statement or act should be characterized as antisemitic arouses great controversy because the sheer accusation of antisemitism can itself function as a taboo: it can be used (or abused) to shut down debate over the conduct of the state of Israel, as if its actions lay beyond all critical scrutiny or could be exempted from the universal standards of international law or human rights. To be sure, this debate is overdetermined in countless ways. On the one hand, a state that arrogates to itself an identity as Jewish will naturally serve as a lightning rod that draws to itself the accumulated antisemitic prejudices of the past. Given the variability of antisemitic discourse, no one should be at all surprised when some critics seem all too ready to single out Israel for selective or disproportionate condemnation in a global context where few (if any) states fully honour international humanitarian codes. On the other hand, as a matter of principle, no state can ever be permitted to exempt itself from criticism. In 1948, when the Jewish people made its Faustian pact with the principles of state power and Israel took up (to

64

quote the sociologist Max Weber) a 'monopoly on the legitimate use of physical force', it necessarily exposed itself to the possibility that it would be condemned for its transgressions, and this includes the possibility that it could be found guilty of crimes against humanity or even genocide.[32] Shutting down that possible charge as *ipso facto* antisemitic does not make Jews any more safe; it only raises the spectre of another theme in the arsenal of antisemitism – namely, that the Jewish state wishes to exempt itself from the moral and political codes that should govern all other states around the globe.

The idea that we must adhere to universal standards that apply to *all* states, even in the midst of war, found one of its earliest exponents in Augustine of Hippo, who was also among the first to formulate the principle that a war is just only if it is conducted in such a way as to leave open the possibility for a future peace. A similar principle appears in Kant's 1795 essay on 'Perpetual Peace'.[33] The Kantian principle also appears nearly verbatim in the statement of solidarity with Israel, published on 13 November 2023 (and co-signed by the philosopher Jürgen Habermas) in which we find the proviso that, for all participants in the current conflict in Israel/ Palestine, 'principles of proportionality, the prevention of civilian casualties and the waging of a war with the prospect of future peace must be the guiding principles.'[34] Needless to say, in the contemporary German political context, the debate over Israel's conduct comes freighted with historical anxiety, and it is hardly surprising if many German citizens still feel that the burden of their own political past inhibits them from expressing any condemnation of Israel. Nor should it surprise us that in this highly polarized context Habermas and his colleagues were widely criticized on the left for a statement that was perceived as one-sided in its support for Israel. Within the community of critical theory itself, opinion on this matter remains divided. It is rather ironic and even unfortunate that the statement's specification of 'guiding principles' was passed over in silence, since it should be altogether obvious that this proviso furnishes the only valid standard by which the international community can judge the actions of Israel in Gaza today. This normative standard recalls the very same spirit of universalism that prompted Adorno to speak of a 'new categorical imperative'. In his 1962 lecture, the concluding injunction that *such a thing must never happen again* expresses an ethical requirement that applies to all peoples and states without exception. It is an ethic that has only grown more urgent with the passage of time.

June 2024

Notes to the Afterword

[1] The DKR is still operative today and consists in more than eighty subgroups. For further information, see www.deutscher-koordinierungsrat.de.

[2] Theodor W. Adorno, 'Zur Bekämpfung des Antisemitismus heute', in *Erziehung vorurteilsfreier Menschen. Ernst Europäische Pädagogenkonferenz von 30 Oktober bis. 3. November 1962 in Wiesbaden* (Frankfurt am Main: Deutscher Koordinierungsrat der Gesellschaften für Christlich-Jüdische Zusammenarbeit, 1963).

[3] Adorno, *Negative Dialektik* (Frankfurt am Main: Suhrkamp, 1966); *Negative Dialectics*, trans. E. B. Ashton (London: Routledge, 1973).

[4] Ibid., here following the translation by Dennis Redmond (2001; see https://platypus1917.org/wp-content/uploads/Negative_Dialectics_Redmond trans2021.pdf).

5   Karl Marx and Fredrich Engels, *The Holy Family, or Critique of Critical Criticism: Against Bruno Bauer and Company*, trans. Richard Dixon (Moscow: Foreign Languages Publishing House, [1845] 1956).

6   Adorno, *Einführung in die Dialektik* (Frankfurt am Main: Suhrkamp, 2010), p. 266; *An Introduction to Dialectics*, trans. Nicholas Walker. (Cambridge: Polity, 2017), p. 188.

7   Ibid; my emphasis.

8   For a recent study that argues for the ongoing partnership between critical theory and psychoanalysis, see Amy Allen, *Critique on the Couch: Why Critical Theory Needs Pyschoanalysis* (New York: Columbia University Press, 2020).

9   Adorno et al., *The Authoritarian Personality* (New York: Harper & Brothers, 1950; rev. edn, London: Verso, 2019), p. 228.

10   Stefan Müller-Doohm, *Adorno: A Biography*, trans. Rodney Livingstone (Cambridge: Polity, 2005), p. 292.

11   On the moral importance of the subject's vulnerability and responsiveness, see Peter Gordon, *A Precarious Happiness: Adorno and the Sources of Normativity* (Chicago: University of Chicago Press, 2024). Also see Estelle Ferrarese, *The Fragility of Concern for Others: Adorno and the Ethics of Care*, trans. Steven Corcoran (Edinburgh: Edinburgh University Press, 2020).

12 Adorno, *Minima Moralia: Reflections from Damaged Life*, trans. Edmund Jephcott (London: Verso, 2005), pp. 42–3.

13 Ibid., pp. 192–3.

14 Sigmund Freud, *Group Psychology and the Analysis of the Ego*, trans James Strachey. (New York: W. W. Norton, [1921] 1990), p. 92.

15 Ibid., p. 82.

16 Adorno et al., *The Authoritarian Personality* (2019), p. 975.

17 In Schiller's 'Ode to Joy', the text of the Ninth Symphony, any person is included in the circle provided he is able to call 'even a single soul his own in this wide world'; that is, the person who is happy in love. 'But he who has none, let him steal weeping from our company.' Inherent in the bad collective is the image of the solitary, and joy desires to see him weep. (Adorno, *Beethoven: The Philosophy of Music*, trans. Edmund Jephcott (Cambridge: Polity, 1998), pp. 32–3)

18 Alexander and Margarete Mitscherlich, *The Inability to Mourn: Principles of Collective Behavior*, trans. Beverly Placzek (New York: Grove Press, 1975).

19 Adorno, *Aspects of the New Right-Wing Extremism* (Cambridge: Polity, 2020).

20 Adorno, *Metaphysics: Concepts and Problems*, trans. Edmund Jephcott (Stanford, CA: Stanford University Press, 2000), p. 115.

21 Stanley Milgram, 'Behavioral Study of Obedience', *Journal of Abnormal and Social Psychology* 67/4 (1963):

371–8. The study came to popular attention with the publication of Milgram's *Obedience to Authority: An Experimental View* (New York: HarperCollins, 1974).

22 Devan Pendas, *The Frankfurt Auschwitz Trial, 1963–1965: Genocide, History, and the Limits of the Law* (Cambridge: Cambridge University Press, 2010), p. 144.

23 As quoted in Rebecca Wittmann, *Beyond Justice: The Auschwitz Trial* (Cambridge, MA: Harvard University Press, 2012), p. 255.

24 Adorno, *Introduction to Sociology*, trans. Edmund Jephcott (Stanford, CA: Stanford University Press, 2002), Lecture Fourteen (2 July 1968), p. 117.

25 Adorno, *Metaphysics: Concepts and Problems*, trans. Edmund Jephcott (Stanford, CA: Stanford University Press, 2000), p. 116.

26 Adorno, *Problems of Moral Philosophy*, trans. Rodney Livingstone (Cambridge: Polity, 2000), p. 167.

27 Adorno, *Erziehung zur Mündigkeit. Vorträge und Gespräche mit Hellmut Becker 1959 bis 1969*, ed. Gerd Kadelbach (Frankfurt am Main: Suhrkamp, 1971).

28 Adorno et al., *The Authoritarian Personality* (2019), p. 971.

29 Shulamith Volkov, 'Antisemitism as a Cultural Code', *Leo Baeck Institute Year Book* 23 (1978), pp. 25–45.

30 On the implications of the word 'again' and the necessity of comparison, see the remarks by the journalist Masha Gessen upon receiving the Hannah Arendt Prize in December 2023. The remarks were published online in *Die Zeit* in both German and English: see www.zeit.de/kultur/2023-12/masha-gessen-rede-hannah-arendt-preis-english.

31 See Peter E. Gordon, 'Why Historical Analogy Matters', *New York Review of Books* (7 January 2020), www.nybooks.com/online/2020/01/07/why-historical-analogy-matters.

32 Human Rights Watch, Amnesty International and the ICC (International Criminal Court) have all contributed to the discussion of Israel's conduct in Gaza and have not shirked from entertaining the accusation of genocide. As Aryeh Neier has noted, 'Netanyahu's assertion that ICC indictments would be antisemitic is indicative of his promiscuous use of antisemitism allegations.' See Aryeh Neier, 'Is Israel Committing Genocide?' *New York Review of Books* (6 June 2024).

33 Immanuel Kant, 'Perpetual Peace: A Philosophical Sketch', in Kant, *Political Writings*, ed. Hans Reiss (Cambridge: Cambridge University Press, 1970), pp. 93–130; see esp. p. 96.

34 See www.normativeorders.net/2023/grundsatze-der-solidaritat/.

About the Authors

Theodor W. Adorno (1903–1969) was a philosopher and sociologist. He was one of the main exponents of critical theory as practised by the Frankfurt School, which emerged from the Institute of Social Research at the University of Frankfurt. In addition, with his lectures, radio broadcasts and publications, he had a formative influence on cultural and intellectual life in post-war Germany.

Peter E. Gordon is the Amabel B. James Professor of History and Faculty Affiliate in the Departments of Government and Philosophy at Harvard University. He is the author of many books, most recently *A Precarious Happiness:*

Adorno and the Sources of Normativity, which was published in German by Suhrkamp Verlag and in English by the University of Chicago Press.